Table Art
PANGO'S

FRUIT AND VEGETABLE CARVINGS

BY: ALFREDO T. PANGO

Amaze guests, friends and family members with photos that will tickle your imagination on how to create a unique table art Presentation.

Made from Real Fruits and Vegetables

7- 2008   Gen Fund $20.⁰⁰

This book was printed in the United States of America.

To order additional copies of this book, contact:
Xlibris Corporation
1-888-795-4274
www.Xlibris.com
Orders@Xlibris.com

Pango's Table Art
5000 Jane St., Suite 1209
North York, Ontario
M3N 2W5
Toronto, Canada

Or

Visit our Web site address: www.pangostableart.ca

DEDICATION

To my beloved parents, Geronimo & Veneranda Pango;

It took me a long time to decide and think that it cost me a lot of thinking, space and time away from you, wishing I could carve my dreams and write my hurts in the sand where winds of forgiveness can blow them away; and instead form a blessing in a stone where no wind can ever erase it.

A cloud does not know why it moves in such a direction and such a speed, but the sky knows all the reasons and patterns behind every cloud. That is why; I am more than confident that you knew in your heart, I have to follow my callings. I love you.

Fred

TABLE OF CONTENTS

Pango's Table Art

A Guide to Create a Professional Quality Fruit and Vegetable Carvings;
Pango's Table Art, fashion a step-by-step instructions about the art of fruit and vegetable Carvings, beginners and professionals will be inspired by the knack of its unique table decoration with the use of common household fruits and veggies, the intricacy of the craft belies simplicity: even beginners can manipulate assorted fruits and vegetables to appear like a magnificent real flower, whimsical animals and other centerpiece that would make the eye glitter in awe.

Pango, has been designing edible table decorations for thirty years, through his artistry, he adds magic and splendor to sweet tables, wine and cheese tables, antipasto bars, hot and cold buffet tables and many other special occasions that requires his craft and artistry. It is the magic of his art that has endeared Pango to thousands of people over the years, as he shares his talent through seminars and demonstrations. Passengers on cruise ships, become spellbound by Pango's artistic arrangement with a typical comments that includes, "I can't believe those, chrysanthemums are really Onions!" "Are those really cabbage leaves?" and "How do you get the leaves to shine like that?"

Pango's Table Art is a response to thousands of people who have asked Pango to share his secrets and skills in carving fruit and vegetables flowers, so here it is with vivid photographs of his most popular carvings, written along are directions on how it is going to be made. Carvings include exotic animals, such as eggplant penguin, fruits and vegetable elephant to be use as centerpiece or showpiece, watermelon monkey, white turnip ostrich and zucchini birds sitting at the center platter with Leek flowers as an equally impressive floral design; like zucchini tulip flowers garnished & decorated at the center of the table, so also the white turnip roses in brilliant Jeweled-tone color. You can also see assorted vegetable flowers, glossy red-and-white cabbage lilies all of which bloom in brilliant colors.

In addition to an easy-to-follow instruction is a beautifully photographed carvings, *Pango's Table Art* also features well-illustrated sections on carving equipment and techniques, as well as suggestions in assembling an elegant buffet table by simply adding a fruit and vegetable carving.

With Pango's Table Art, entertaining takes a whole lot of new meaning.

How to Dye Bamboo Skewers Green

3 packs   Bamboo skewers 12" (100 pcs. per pack)
2 cups   Green food coloring
1 cup   White vinegar
1 cup   Water

Procedure

1. Prepare 3 packs of 12" inches bamboo skewers (100pcs. each bag).
2. Prepare a flat container (12 x 9 inches or larger so long as there is enough space to accommodate skewers.

3. Mix one cup of water to a cup of white vinegar, add two cups of Green food coloring and mix well.
4. Place bamboo skewers into the green liquid solution.
5. Soak for at least two nights, for the green solution to absorb.
6. After the soaking period, wash off with water extra and unnecessary food coloring.
7. Let dry by using a clean cloth or paper towel and set aside.

How to Prepare Floral Vase

Flower vase should be prepared ahead of time

- 1pc.   Watermelon
- 1pc.   Pineapple
- 1pack bamboo skewers 12" (100 pcs. in a bag)
- Bunch of heather leaves or any leaves

Preparation

1. Use a chef's knife to cut watermelon into two, cross wise.
2. Cut Pineapple into two, cross wise. Utilize the other half and put it in the center of your Watermelon vase.

Note: The remaining half of your Watermelon should be set-aside for other purposes such as Fruit salad mixture and dressing for other fruit refinement.

3. Put eight or more skewers enough to hold it in a standing position.

4. Attach skewers side by side, alternately.

5. Insert skewers, starting from the top of the pineapple through the inner center of watermelon, break the skewers if long.

6. Use paring knife to carve small V-shape around the edge of the Watermelon, without damaging the pineapple base by carving the Melon's skin using a flower cutter for any floral design that would make it look presentable as well. As shown in the photo illustration.

7. Use heather leaves or any vegetable leaf to give a floral design to Watermelon's base.

Preparation of the Unflavored Gelatin

- 2cups   unflavored gelatin powder (add gelatin powder depending on how big the carving is)
- 4cups   cold water
- 1pitcher hot water (boiled)

Miscellaneous
- Stainless bowl (large)
- Hand stirring whiz
- White Paper napkin for sanitation purposes

Procedure

1. Use a large stainless bowl, for the gelatin mixture.

2. Prepare one pitcher of hot water.

3. Prepare two cups of unflavored gelatin powder.

4. Prepare 4 cups of cold water, hand stirring whiz & few white paper napkins.

5. Pour the gelatin powder in a large stainless bowl.

6. Add four cups of cold water into the gelatin, stir until powder dissolves.

7. Add one pitcher of hot water, mix the solution until gelatin powder turns sticky.

8. Use clean towel to get rid of the tiny bubbles from the liquid solution.

9. Leave it for a few minutes to cool down solution.

Process and importance of gelatin solutions on all fruit and vegetable flower carvings

1. Start dipping your fruits or vegetable flowers into the gelatin solution when it is still in liquid form. Cover all area/parts of all flowers that need's a gelatin topcoat.

2. Gelatin is necessary for all flower carvings to add vibrancy, color protection and creating shiny coat to your fruit and vegetable flowers making it look more like a real flower bouquets.

Note

Watch a closer look at your gelatin solution; always keep it in its liquid form.

Keep stirring to prevent it from clogging, if it happens add some hot water and stir again.

The Artist behind the craft – Alfredo Tambis Pango

Alfredo T. Pango is a talented chef, food artist who have had catered the refine taste of patrons of the world's best hotels cruise ships, Clubs and well-known restaurants. During his thirty years of food service and pleasing the eyes of contented patrons, he continued to sweeten their palate. "Pango" as commonly called, has perfected the art of his unique style in making an exquisitely beautiful flowers carved and garnished with different kinds of fruit and vegetables that would look like real than reel.

A native Filipino and Cebuano at heart, but with a soul of a wonderer for Pango is a well traveled Artist, he loves to serve by enchanting people from all walks of life with his art that is polished by time, dedication and handwork in response to his calling, Pango has traveled the world free, aboard the Luxury cruise-ship lines as chef de partie, chef de garde manager, and chef buffet man and first pantry man.

For several years, he has dedicated his service on a Norwegian Cruise Liner (NCL) aboard the SS Norway, one of the world's largest cruise ships, so with the MS Sunward II. In addition to his glamorous career, Pango has appeared in several television shows, including Toronto's CITY TV, morning news programs the Breakfast Television and Nota Bene, an Italian-Canadian Broadcasting program. He has been featured as front cover of Toronto's Italian newspaper Lo Specchio; also a member of the Chefs' Italian Association. Pango has also given public demonstrations about his food art at numerous bridal conventions-the Metro Toronto Convention Center, the Toronto Exhibition Place Convention Center and the Toronto Pearson International Airport Convention Center.

Colleague - Scott Kruger

   I have been working with Pango for over eight years now and let me disclose what I have seen from his amazing works over the time. My role in this partnership is to help support Pango whichever way I can, as we attend to several clients.

I was born in Edmonton Alberta, moved to Toronto at a very young age and the entire time since I've been involved in the food industry and I was working at restaurants, Banquet halls and hotels, where I learned the trade.

My role includes, being a bartender, waiter and food purchaser-receiver and preparations, cook and event coordinator. My career basically mirrors that of Pango for the past eight years. We have an excellent personal and business relationship that helps the business grow.

Description of Tools

Chef Knife
This cutting instrument consists of one or more sharpened edge blades, attached to handle to cut with a knife.

Curved Paring Knife
A curved paring knife carves a continuous line having no straight paths.

Paring Knife
The paring knife is flexible for carving, peeling delicate Decoration; particularly fruit and vegetables.

Melon Baler
This tool is used to carve melon fruit to form into balls, large/small size to create circles by 1 or 3 centimeters.

V-shape Food Carver Decorator (3/8")
This tool could create a small V-shape to fruits or veggies for any decoration. Build into fruits or vegetable base.

V-shape Food Carver Tool
A fixable tool used to create V-shapes for fruits and vegetables.

Design Cutters
Unique life-long designed cutters, patterned from an artistic hand crafted stainless steel, used for fruits and vegetables decoration.

- *Flower-shape cutter*
- *Star-shaped cutter etc.*

Brush
This tool is used to brush garnishing.

Vegetable Peeler
This tool is designed for peeling fruit and vegetable skin.

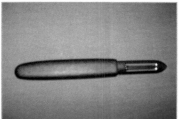

Scissors
A double-edge cutting instrument with blades fastened together with a bolt.

Long Carving Knife
This cutting instrument consists of one or more sharp-edged blade, attached to cut and slice.

Edible Carving Displays

Assorted Vegetable Flowers

You can carve and create any types of fruits and vegetables
to form a flower bouquet or animal kingdom that will be
used as centerpiece or showpieces

Philippine Chayote Frogs

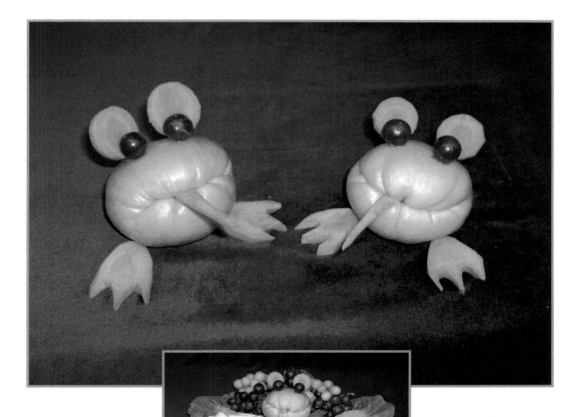

Chayote frog at the center of
a cold cuts platter with garnishing

Tools

- Chef Knife
- Paring Knife
- Curve Paring Knife
- Peeler
- Marker (washable)

Fruits and vegetables to be needed

- 1 pc.   Chayote (vegetable)
- 1 pc.   Carrot (large)
- 2 pcs.   Red grapes
- 1 pack   Toothpicks (round shape)

Steps and procedure in making a chayote frog

1. Use fresh chayote vegetable, make sure quality is good.
2. Use a chef's knife to create a slanting cut at about an inch thick from the Chayote's bottom, that is to provide a stable base for your Chayote frog.
3. After providing the base, keep it aside for later use.
4. Get a piece of carrot and use a peeler to skin it off.

Steps on how to create chayote frogs eye, eyebrows and tongue

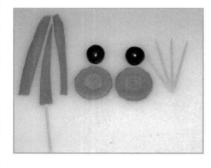

1. Two pieces of whole red grapes for the eyes.
2. With chef's knife, slice two-rounded portion of carrot at about .03 cm thick, for the eyebrows.
3. Cut a slice of carrot in long /pyramid shape at about .03 cm. thick to create a tongue.
4. Attach toothpick at the bottom of the carrot pyramid to form a tongue, be careful not to break the carrots and pattern it as shown in the Photo illustration
5. Prepare five pieces of toothpicks to assemble.

Steps in creating web feet

1. Use a large carrot, a peeler to get rid of the skin.
   Slice two pieces of carrot in slanting/diagonal cut at about .04 cm. thick.
2. Use a washable marker to trace two U-shape patterns along the tip of the carrot.

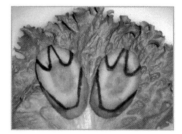

Column A

Column B

3. Use curved paring knife to make out the U-shape pattern of the Webfeet as shown in the picture below or you can create any design of Carrot webfeet.
4. Once done, wash it with water and soak carrot webfeet, eyebrows and the carrot tongue.

Steps on how to assemble the chayote veggie frog

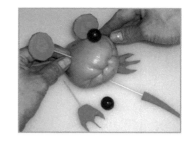

1. Bring about the chayote vegetable you have set aside for the body of the Chayote frog.
2. Attach two round carrots on top of the chayote to form the Carrot Eyebrows, since we do not have bolts to hold them in place we use toothpick.
3. Insert toothpicks on both sides, right in front of the carrot Eyebrows; leaving a space for the grapes to sit in.
4. Insert two red grapes in front of the carrot eyebrows, to create the eyes of the frog as shown in the photo illustration.

5. Attach carrot webfeet at the bottom of the chayote vegetable and place toothpick on it to hold.
6. Attach, long sliced carrot at the mouth's center to create Chayote frog's tongue, insert toothpick to hold instead of using bolts and screws to secure it.

7. Your Philippine chayote frog is now ready to be displayed on cold cuts platter, Antipasto plates and other table settings or whatever purposes it may serve. See photo illustrations page 15.

Steps and procedure on how to form fruits and vegetable base

1. Prepare fruits and vegetables, either orange or potato, preferably large in size.
2. With a knife, cut the bottom of the fruit to form its base.
3. Prepare three pieces of large green curly leaves or any vegetable leaf.

4. Cover the top of the fruit with green leaves, use toothpicks to secure them and attach the core of the leaves as shown in the illustration.

5. Prepare an oval platter or any form, put it in the center or use it as base.

6. Cover the platter with green curly leaves, as shown in the illustration.

7. Then, organize the cold cuts (sliced turkey) or assorted fruits & vegetable display; before putting the Chayote frog or any carvings you prefer. That's to complete the arrangement for base & organize the tray with leaves, and it is now ready to be a centerpiece/showpiece presentation.

Pear Mouse

Pear mouse, sitting at the top center of assorted fruits on a platter

Tools

- Chef's Knife
- Curve Paring Knife or Paring knife
- Peeler

Fruits and vegetable needed

- 1pc.   Pear fruit (color/optional)
- 1pc.   Carrot (regular)
- 2pcs.   Cloves
- 1pack Toothpicks (round)
- 1pc.   Red grapes

Steps and procedure on how to make a pear mouse

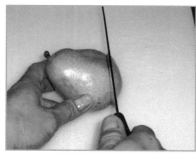

1. Choose a piece of pear fruit of good quality.
2. Use a paring knife to cut off base at about ¼ of an inch in an Angular position to make your mouse stand skyward when arranged.

Steps on how to create pear carrot ears and the carrot foot

1. After carving the base, engraved both sides-top head of pear fruit, using a paring knife to shave off meat, at about 1cm. deep. Large enough to insert the carrot ears on top. Shown in the photo illustration below.

2. Use red grapes and put it on the upper tip of toothpick as tail.
3. Also two cloves for the eyes.
4. Use carrot of regular size and a peeler to discard carrot skin.
5. Use a knife, to cut two-carrot slice at the bottom, .03–. 04cm. thick in an elongated/slanting pattern for the feet.
6. With paring knife cut V—shape patterns for the carrot feet.
7. Cut another two-carrot slice at the bottom, .03–. 04cm. thick in an elongated/slanting pattern, for the ears.
8. With curve paring knife cut the carrot in a pointed oval shape for the carrot ears or you may create any desired form.

Steps on how to assemble the pear mouse

1. Take the pear fruit you have had prepared for the mouse.
2. Insert two slices of carrot on the space you made for the ears. Use toothpicks to secure it.
3. Insert cloves in front of the carrot ears to form the eyes.
4. At the back of the pear fruit, insert a toothpick with a red grape.
5. Secure carrot feet by attaching a toothpick on it, to hold.
6. You may now display it on fruit platter/table or antipasto plate as Centerpiece/showpiece.

3436600023092

Melon Doggie

Centerpiece

Tools

- Chef Knife or Long Carving Knife
- Paring Knife
- Curve Paring Knife
- Peeler

Fruits and Vegetables needed

- 1pc.   Honeydew melon (large/oblong)
- 1pc.   Honeydew melon (small/round)
- 6pcs.   Carrots (regular)
- 1pc.   Orange
- 50grams Red grapes
- 2pcs.   Pineapple leaves or any vegetable leaf
- 1pc.   Eggplant (large)
- 1-bag   Bamboo skewers (12", 100 pcs. in a bag)
- 1 pack   Toothpicks (round)

Simple steps and procedure on how to make a melon doggie's head

1. Use a round-shaped honeydew melon of good quality.
2. Establish a base by using a chef's knife to cut the melon by an inch, top or bottom side.
3. You have to use a sketch-carving tool with washable ink on it. Trace two circles in between the upper top head of the melon to establish the eyes, as shown in the photo illustration.
4. Form a bat shape just under the eyes to emphasize the mouth.

5. A chef's knife is needed to shred an inch along the circled line, cutting it in a side-by-side formation to establish the eyes.

6. It is necessary to use a curved paring knife to manipulate the bat shape mouth formation, as shown in the picture illustration above.

Steps on how to create the ears

1. In an upright manner, slice the melon's skin without damaging the meat in conveying the ear formation and do not forget to use a Chef's knife to do the trick.

2. Once done with the eyes, mouth and the ears, you may set it aside for the final presentation.

Steps and ways how to create a melon doggie

Hat Take a piece of eggplant large size, use chef's knife and cut at the center of the eggplant, incise eggplant by an inch thick or any size desired. Use an orange cut in half to be used for the hat.
The remaining half of the orange will be use for other purposes.

Neck Cut another slice of eggplant; chop the skinny part by an inch thick using a chef's knife to create an even slice.

Eyes You will need additional two-pieces of carrot at .03 cm. thick, for the Eyes.

Pupils You will need two pieces red grapes cut by an inch.

Buttons Use carrot; discard skin by using a peeler. The skinny part should be cut in a rounded form in about .03 cm. thick to serve as button base. You will also need three slices of rounded Carrot cut in halves, along with three red grapes for the buttons.

Tongue You can utilize the remaining carrots to establish a diagonal cut almost oval in shape around .04 to .05 cm. thick to be used as tongue.

Tie This is where we need the pineapple leaves to make our tie; there is a need to use every artistic inclination we have to make it look real and presentable.

Steps and preparation to create arms and legs

1. You will need four pieces of carrots. Discard skin by using a peeler.
2. Use a knife to cut carrot's bottom in a slanting manner.
3. The small of carrot will be sliced in a different way, should be cut straight for perfect positioning when assembled.

Steps and procedure in making the feet

1. Use carrot and peel off skin. Use the bottom and slice four equal cut at about .04 cm. thick, form five V-shapes along the side that will be used later to form the feet or any shape you desire.

Steps on how to prepare the body

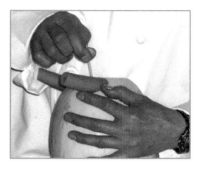

1. Choose a large oblong-shaped honeydew melon of good quality, with no bruises on the skin.
2. To gain access on a stable base, you have to cut the top/bottom part of melon by an inch.
3. After creating the base, it is now advisable to establish the arms and legs. You will have to attach the sliced carrots one at a time. Two of which will be positioned in the topside, while the other two will be put in the lower part of your melon doggie. Since we are not using any metal screw and bolts, we have to use toothpicks to hold the parts together.

Simplified steps on how to assemble

1. Attach the rounded carrot on every open point of the arms to give emphasis on the hands, while doing the same process for the feet, you should always use toothpicks to hold it in place.

2. You will now need the pineapple leaves, locked them together with a sliced carrot and a small red grape to draw it to a close.
3. Continue the process with the rest of the carrots and grapes, excluding the pineapple leaf that serves its purpose as a tie
4. To establish a permanent neck, you have to attach a sliced eggplant, Another toothpick is needed to secure it in place.

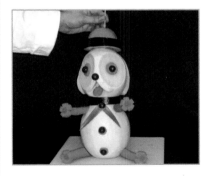

5. Attach the melon head over the top of the sliced eggplant, you will then need a bamboo skewers to secure the head, toothpick is too weak for the purpose.
6. Attach sliced carrot to form the eyes. Use toothpicks to hold and be careful not to puncture the eye.
7. Insert two halves of red grapes at the mid of your rounded Carrot to bring about the pupils.

8. Now the tricky part, you will need a toothpick, station it right between the eyes with a red grape at its tip to make out the reddish nose of your melon doggie.

9. For the hat, you will need bamboo skewers to hold the inch thick eggplant and the half sized Orange cut crosswise.

10. Attach a piece of toothpick at the top of the orange. Insert the grapes to complete the entire hat.

11. An oval shaped carrot at .03 cm. thick should be stacked in the doggie's mouth to have the sight of its pinkish tongue.

12. To bring your creation into life there are center of tables, Sweet tables waiting or any occasion.

Watermelon Monkey

Tools

- Chef Knife or Long Carving Knife
- Paring Knife
- Curve Paring Knife
- Peeler
- Marker (washable) or Sketch Carving Tool

Fruits and Vegetables

- 1pc.   Watermelon (reg./seedless)
- 2pcs.   Honeydew melon (large)
- 1pc.   Cantaloupe melon (Round, Medium size)
- 4pcs.   Yellow squash (Large)
- 2pcs.   White turnips (large)
- 2pcs.   Carrots (large)
- 50grms Red grapes (large)
- 1pc.   Orange
- 1bag   Bamboo skewers 12" (100 pcs. in a bag)
- 1pack   Toothpicks (round)

Steps and procedure of preparations

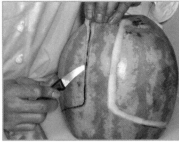

1. Use a watermelon of good quality, without skin pigmentations.
2. With the use of a chef's knife, cut the top/bottom of the watermelon to form a base to make your watermelon monkey stand upright.
3. Use marker or sketch carving tool to trace watermelons skin to define the clothes formation to your watermelon monkey.
4. Use tip of your curved paring knife to cut the marked line without puncturing the inner meat for easy removal.
5. Use a chef's knife or long carving knife to peel off watermelon's skin until white meat is exposed, as shown in the photo illustrations, found in page 27.

Arms and Legs Preparations

1. Four pieces of yellow squash for the arms and legs. How?
2. Use yellow squash, and cut it in half or in two, in a slanting manner. (Length and side is optional)
3. The remaining yellow squash will be used to complete the arms and legs.

Hands and Feet Preparation

1. Two pieces of large white turnips of good quality use a peeler to discard the skin.
2. Use the center of your peeled turnip and cut two round shapes at about .05 inch thick.
3. The same procedure of cutting and of the same thickness for the remaining turnip.
4. As you cut the turnips you can form it into a hand and feet, as show in the photo illustrations.
5. Use a paring knife/curve paring knife to make at least four equal sections to the sliced turnips. Make sure you do not include the inner part to define hand formation. Hand design is optional you can create any design out of an ordinary vegetables or fruits.
6. The remaining last two slices would be used as feet, carve it by using a paring knife or curve paring knife just like the hand.

Hat and Ears Preparation

1. Use a cantaloupe melon, cut and slice it at about an inch thick, also an orange cut into two that would serve as the hat. Set aside for later usage.
2. Get your honeydew melon, use a knife to cut both ends of melon at least two slices at .04 inch thick for the ears.

How to make a ribbon or bow tie

1. Use a large sized carrot, peel off skin and discard.
2. Use a chef's knife to cut the carrots bottom. Slice the carrot at about .05 inch thick and shape it into square.
3. Carved carrot by using a curved paring knife to make a ribbon form.
4. After carving the ribbon, cut up the edge to create a defined line to bring out a mystical look on your make-believed ribbon.

How to make Buttons and Pocket

1. Another large carrot is needed, peel off skin and discard.
2. Use a knife to cut three round shaped-carrots and two red grapes cut into two for the buttons.
3. Cut another two round slice at about .03 cm thick for the eyes.
4. Cut carrot in a slanting manner at about .03 cm thick for the tongue.
5. With the knife, cut the carrot in a slanting form at .03–. 04 cm thick, to create a carrot pocket. Design and size of pocket and buttons is also optional.

Steps on how to create the head

1. Medium size and preferably round in shape honeydew melon and in good quality is necessary.
2. Use a chef's knife to cut the bottom part of the melon by .05 inch and top part of the melon cut .03 inch thick to prepare a base.
3. With a marker or a sketch-carving tool, trace two circles (large/round) on the melon skin to create an eye.

4. Using a chef's knife you can remove a point of an inch along the eye line, Cutting side by side to form the eyes. as shown in the picture illustration p 23, Second column.
5. In between the eye or just under it, draw a bat form to elaborate the mouth formation, as shown in the picture illustration p 23, 1ˢᵗ column
6. Use a curve paring knife to define the bat shape out of its line.

7. On the side corner of the eyes, draw a C-shape. use curve paring knife

   cut an elongated C-form for the ears. Keep on the side. Use for later. Next steps.

How to assemble

1. Ready your watermelon monkey.
2. Attach four pieces of yellow squash on the top and bottom side of the body of your Watermelon monkey, to form the arms and legs. Use toothpicks to hold both arms and legs together.

3. Use the prepared turnips hand and feet/shoe.
4. Attach them on squash tip, as shown in the picture, use toothpicks to keep it in place.
5. Carrot ribbon will be place on the top center, with the use of a toothpick, to hold.
6. Attach half red grapes on top of carrot a ribbon.
7. Follow the sequence with the rounded carrots with grapes on top of it to form the buttons.

8. The right side corner will be saved for the pocket.

9. Take the melon head you have had prepared, attach the melon skin on the eye corner, to form Ears and use toothpicks to hold.

10. Position the melon head on top of the watermelon body; be sure to use bamboo skewers to hold it in place, toothpicks are too vulnerable for it to stand the weight.

11. Place the rounded carrots to complete the eye formation with red grapes on it.

12. In between the eyes insert toothpick that will hold the grape that would serve as the nose.

13. Use a bamboo skewer to hold the cantaloupe melon and the sliced orange for the hat.

14. Do not forget to attach the carrot tongue with the use of a toothpick.

15. Buffet and sweet tables, so much so antipasto bars are waiting for the watermelon Monkey; to grace every diner's palate and visual appetites.

Watermelon Wise Old Owl

It's party time and wise old bird is dressed in style, ready to add pizza to your buffet and dinner table.

Tools
- Chef Knife
- Paring Knife
- Curve Paring Knife
- V-shaped Carving Tool
- Peeler

Fruits and Vegetables needed

- 1pc.   Watermelon long (regular or seedless)
- 2–3pcs.   Carrots (large)
- 2pcs.   Maraschino cherries
- 500gms.   Red grapes
- 1pc.   Pineapple
- 1pc.   Lemon
- 1pack   Toothpicks, round shape
- 1bag   Bamboo skewers 12" (100pcs. in a bag)

Simple step and procedure of preparation

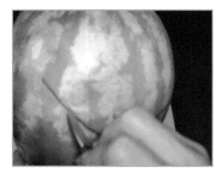

1. Choose a watermelon, which is oval in shape and of good quality.
2. Cut its bottom an inch thick to make a stable base.
3. Stand the watermelon upright, use a sketch-carving tool with a washable ink on it to trace a half-moon shape, just above the upper One-third of the melons body.
4. Use the pointed tip of the curve paring knife to mark the line by an inch before peeling the skin.

Steps on how to cut wing manually

1. With the use of a chef's knife or long carving knife, shave off the Watermelon skin in an upright cut on both sides, at about ¼ thick of an inch., In preparation for the wings of your wise watermelon Owl.

2. Use a chef's knife or long carving knife to peel off center skin. Expose the white rind or first layer meat like the one seen on the picture.

Steps on how to create the wings

1. At the edge of the peeled watermelon skin, create small V-shapes to emphasize the wing formation
2. A paring knife is necessary to create the small V-shapes also at the front side to form the feathers.

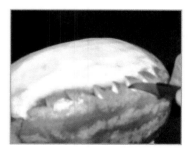

Manual step to create an eye and eyebrows

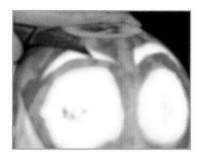

1. At the upper center of the watermelon's face, make two distinct circles using a chef's knife to cut skin at about 3cm. thick for the eye cutting it side by side in a slanting formation.
   Be sure that it is placed evenly.
2. Right above the eyes, use curve paring knife to carve two "Cs" positioned facedown, where you insert a sliced carrot to create the eyebrows.

Steps on how to manipulate an Owl's figure

1. Use a large carrot, especially the bottom part. Peel off skin and discard.
2. Cut carrot forming two oval shapes in about 3cm. thick for the eyes. You will also need red Grapes, cut an inch for the pupils.
3. Another three pieces of rounded carrots at .03 cm thick is needed and so also maraschino Cherries, cut into two cross wise for our carrot buttons.
4. To create a carrot web feet, see photo illustrations found on page 16, column A & B
   Note: Slice carrots in a slanting manner to produce an oval shape that would serve as the carrot webfeet,
5. Use the lemon and sliced two lemon rings at .05 cm wide for the eyeglasses.
   Using a paring knife to discard the lemon fruit meat.
6. Get another piece of carrot, peel off its skin and use only its tip for the nose.
7. Fresh pineapple is necessary for the head; you must cut it off at about two inches thick.
   Make sure to keep the leaves and some fruit meat for the feathers.
8. Set aside two pieces of pineapple leaves for the tie.
9. Prepare toothpicks and bamboo skewers to hold body parts together.

How to prepare the carrot eyebrows

1. Another piece of carrot is needed preferably large in size without skin.
2. You will need a chef's knife to cut two elongated shape in a slanting manner at about 3cm. thick.
3. Use curve paring knife to style a small V-shapes along the edge of the carrot without puncturing the inner meat, as shown in the pictures below.

Creation of a carrot eyebrow

Easy to follow steps on how to assemble the Watermelon Wise Owl

1. Stand the watermelon upright and attach all the necessary body parts.
2. Attach the oval shape carrot at the upper center of the watermelons face to form the eyes. Use toothpicks to secure it in place and insert a grape for eye emphasis.

3. Right under the eyes, secure a space, enough to attach the carrot tip to produce a distinguished nose.
4. On top of the Owl's head just above the eyes, attach the carrot eyebrows. Toothpicks are of great help to secure and hold it in place.
5. You will now need the pineapple leaves, interlock both ends and attach a sliced carrot to have a tie form. Use toothpick to hold. Repeat the process to the rest of the carrot buttons down to the mid center of the owl's body to get a perfect button formation. Excluding the Pineapple leaf one layer is more than enough.
6. The pineapple head with leaves on top of it should be placed above the owl's head for hair purposes. You may use six pieces of toothpicks or a skewer, to hold it in place.

7. Red grapes can be utilized as feathers or hair.

8. The finishing touches would be our carrot web feet styled to stay on the bottom.

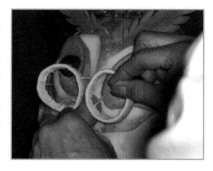

9. Don't forget the lemon ring eyeglasses.

   Attach lemon ring eyeglasses and use toothpicks to hold it.

   Insert a toothpick at the center of the lemon to hold it together.

   Insert another toothpick at the corner side of lemon ring and attach to

   the carrot nose to form an eyeglass.

10. You now have an elegant owl, so wise that it could almost read the art of vegetable carving that

    makes buffet tables more palatable.

Twin Lemon Fish

Twin lemon fish, setting at the side corner of an antipasto di-mare
with garnishing

Tools

- Chef Knife
- Paring Knife
- Curve Paring Knife
- Peeler

Fruits and Vegetables needed

- 1pc.   Lemon (any size)
- 2pcs.   Cloves
- 2pcs.   Carrots (reg. size)
- 1pc.   Red apple
- 1pc.   Cantaloupe melon
- 6pcs.   Red grapes
- 1pack   Toothpicks

Steps and procedure of preparation

1. Use a fresh lemon with no skin pigmentations.
2. To manipulate a stable base, you have to cut the bottom by an inch thick.
3. Use a paring knife to cut a V–shapes at the lemons tip to create the mouth your lemon fish.
4. Slice lemon at two cm. deep and at four cm. long, in preparation for the fins. Do the same process for side fins, without puncturing the juice sack.

5. Slice a two cm. deep and a four cm. long from the back of your lemon fruit, to create a space for the tail.

Manipulating a flame shape fins

1. Use a regular size carrot that is skin clean.
2. Use a chef's knife to maneuver a slanting cut at about .05 cm. thick to your carrot fins. You have a free reign on how to design a fin of your choice.
3. Use the curve paring knife in styling your fins into a "Flame Shape".

How to create the Carrot tail

1. You can also utilize the remaining carrot for the tail.
2. With curve paring Knife you can form five or more equal strings as fish tail. You could also create your own tail design or you could just follow the procedure in making a carrot tail. See photo illustration.

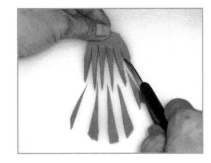

Simple steps to assemble a lemon fish

1. Prepare the lemon body for the lemon fish.
2. Insert carrot fins of lemon fish, one by one.
3. Squeeze the lemon lightly as you insert carrot fins. Be careful on how to handle the lemon without breaking the juice sack.

4. Insert carrot tail at the back of the lemon.

5. As soon as fins and tail are secured in place, use the pointed tip of skewers to puncture a hole in between the front of carrot Fins make enough space for the cloves to get in and establish the eyes.

6. Now the twin lemon fish are ready for display on your antipasto di-mare, see photo on p. 36

Eggplant Baby Owl

Center of a fruit platter table

Tools

- Chef Knife
- Paring Knife or Curve Paring Knife
- Peeler
- Sketch Carving Tool

Necessary fruits and Vegetables

- 1pc.   Eggplant (large)
- 1–2pcs.   Carrots (medium)
- 130gms. Red grapes
- 1 pc.   Orange
- 1 pc.   Lemon
- 1 pack   Toothpicks (round)
- 1 pack   Bamboo skewers (100 pcs. in a bag)

Procedure on how to make an eggplant baby owl

HOW TO CREATE THE FACE AND BODY

1. Use a large eggplant, preferably with good skin quality.
2. Use a chef's knife to chop the thin handle of eggplant to form a base.
3. Stand the eggplant upright and cut a half-moon shape on the upper face by the use a sketch-carving toll, to outline the face.
4. Use the pointed tip of the paring knife to mark the line by a cm. just below the face before peeling the skin off.

Steps to wing creation

1. Use a chef's knife or a long carving knife to create an upright cut in the Eggplant's skin in its frontal view; to magnify wing formation of your Eggplant Baby Owl.
2. Be mindful to stop just above the face, a deeper cut will damage the form.
3. Use a peeler or a sharp edged knife to shave off skin right below the Halfmoon formation.

4. Do not forget to squeeze fresh lemon to the exposed skin so that undue discoloration will not happen or wash the entire body with water after peeling.

How to form the face

1. Use a chef's knife or a long carving knife to remove three cm. thick of eggplant meat in a circled form, it should be positioned side by side just to have a physical eye formation of the baby owl or any formation carving the eyes, as you desire.
2. Above the eyes, use a curve paring knife to manipulate a "C" formation, of which is done facedown to extend room for the carrot eyebrows.

For feather formation, you just have to use a curve paring knife to engrave a V shape form, along the side's edge.

Preparation on how to create the owl's body

Prepare the hat-	Use an orange to form a ring with the use of a chef's knife. Slice it at about .05 inch thick or you can make it a little thicker. Get also a lemon, cut cross wise.
Hair creation-	Bunch of red grapes about 120 grams or more, to be used as hairs.
Carrot eyebrows-	(See illustration page 34.)
Carrot eyes-	Use peeled carrot, sliced at 3cm. thick in round or oval form & red grapes cut at an inch to form the pupil of the eyes.
Carrot nose-	Use carrot tip, cut in slanting manner, size and length is optional.
Carrot buttons-	Cut three pieces rounded carrot at .03 cm. thick, along with grapes in halves to modify the buttons.
Web feet-	To create carrot webfeet, see illustration on page 16 columns A and B.

Steps in Assembling the Baby Owl

1. Attach round carrot in between the eggplant to create the eyes.
2. Attach grapes over the top of the carrot to form the pupils to complete Eye formation.
3. Positioned carrot tip in between the eyes to establish a manifestation of a nose.
4. Put the carrot eyebrows right above the eyes, use toothpicks to secure it in place.
5. Follow the process of positioning buttons with a use of a toothpick.
6. Web feet should be inserted at the bottom of the eggplant, use toothpicks to hold.
7. Attach sliced orange .05 inch thick and so much so is the lemon of which is cut cross wise to complete the hat formation. Attach 90 grams of red grapes on each corner side of the eggplant Baby owl and use toothpicks to hold.
8. Fruit platters, center tables and many other buffet tables are waiting for your Elegant Baby Owl.

Note: Standard fruit and veggie base (See instruction p.17)

1. Secure your base at the center of the platter or whatever plates you are going to use, Use green leaves as matting of your fruits and vegetables. Use toothpicks to hold.

2. Then organize the fruits and vegetables you want to use for additional elegance and style. There is thousands of exotic and elegant way of mastering your creative side, carving your fruits and vegetables to add palatability and glamour, an inch away to your tongue palate, to fascinate not only your taste buds but also your eyes.

Eggplant Penguin

If you want to party and have some fun, well, you have to bring this cool dude out in the sun.

Centerpiece of an antipasto plate with grilled eggplant

Tools

- Chef's knife
- Paring Knife
- Curve Paring Knife
- Peeler

Fruits and Vegetables to be needed

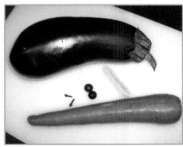

- 1pc.   Eggplant (large)
- 2pcs.   Carrots (medium and large)
- 4pc.   Red grapes (small)
- 2pcs.   Cloves
- 2pcs.   Pineapple leaves
- 1pack   Toothpicks, round shape

The art of preparing an eggplant Penguin

To produce an eggplant penguin that would be suitable for display in platters around buffet tables, center tables and other special occasions that cater the art of fruit and vegetable carving then start with a simple eggplant.

1. Select a large eggplant of good quality with a slight body curve.
2. Use a chef's knife to cut an inch from the bottom of the Eggplant; to manipulate a stable/permanent base to your eggplant Penguin.
3. To carve the wings you can just follow the steps and illustrations found on page 40 on steps to create the wing.

4. Cut two circles on the upper portion of the eggplant to have an eye formation.
5. It would be easy to make a wing for your eggplant Penguin you can look at illustration on page 40.
6. Don't forget to squeeze fresh lemon around the exposed area of your eggplant to avoid unwanted discoloration or wash entire eggplant with water.

Steps on how to create the beak

1. Use a large carrot, peel off skin and discard. Use the lower tip of carrot to form the beak. Size of the beak will depend on how big is your eggplant and how would you want it to look like. Freedom of expression by carving is a must.

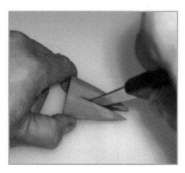

How to make a bow tie from a carrot

1. Utilize the remaining carrot to form a carrot bow tie and webfeet.
   Carrot bow tie, see photo illustration p. 29
   Carrot webfeet see photo illustration p. 16 (column A & B)

How to assemble

1. Use the eggplant body for your Penguin; attach the carrot beak, use toothpick for it to hold.

2. Attach the carrot ribbon or bow tie, preferably with pineapple leaves to complete the tie formation.

3. You will need a rounded slice of carrot with half slice of grape on top of it, to have a physical button appearance while using a toothpick to hold it, in place. Don't forget to insert cloves for the eyes.

4. Place the carrot webfeet at the eggplant's bottom for the feet, use toothpicks to secure them in place.

5. Your eggplant Penguin is now ready to grace any antipasto plates with grilled eggplant around it or you can display the eggplant penguin in any food presentations see photo picture p 43.
   Steps and procedure on how to form fruits and vegetable base see instruction p. 17

White Turnip Ostriches

Tools

- Chef's Knife
- Paring Knife
- Curve Paring Knife
- Peeler
- Potato Baler (medium)
- V-shape Carving Tool 3/8 inch

List of fruits and Vegetables

- 3pcs.   White turnips (large, medium and regular)
- 2pc.   Fresh baby carrot (regular)
- 1pc.   Red beets or potato (large)
- 2pcs.   Cloves
- 3pcs.   Green bamboo sticks (7 inches and thick)
- 1pc.   Green leaves
- 1pack   Toothpicks (round)

The art of preparing a Turnip Ostrich

How to prepare the body of the Ostrich

1. Three round turnips of good quality will suffice, peel off skin and discard.
2. Form a V-shape on your turnip using a food-carving tool to create a curved side-linings to entice an artful design worth looking.

3. At back of your turnip cut an angular strip in preparation for your tail. (.05 inch deep cut found in the column)
4. You have to simply follow the procedure found in the illustrations.
5. Make your chef's knife and paring knife handy for easy and smooth carving.
6. Do not limit your creativity on what is seen on the picture, you can sire a new breed of designs and vegetable carvings, that is what we call art.

Steps for wing formation

1. As shown below, cut turnips in a rounded oval form, for at least. 05cm. thick.
2. Using a washable marker, trace the wings along the sliced turnips before you slice and carve it to perfection, make your paring knife handy for the sculpting of your wings.

3. Before going to the next step, do not forget to wash off the ink with water.

Ways on how to prepare a tale

1. Bring about the prepared turnip, trace it with a washable marker to establish ostrich's tail formation, in an equal proportion of at least five to six strips as shown in the picture illustration.
2. Don't forget to wash away the ink before you assemble every body parts.

A way to prepare the head

1. The last turnip will serve as you ostrich's head; then you have to use a potato baler to carve it.

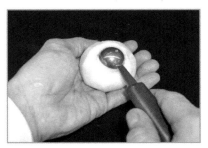

Beak preparation

1. Use a fresh carrot, peel off skin and use the thin tip part for the beak.
2. Size and beak formation will depend on how you want it to look like.
3. It is a must that you soak the beak in a bowl of ice-cold water for it to open up like a real ostrich's beak.

Insert the carrot beak

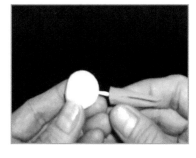

4. After forming the turnip head and carrot beak, attach it with the use of a toothpick without damaging it.
5. Insert the carrot beak at the center of the turnip head ostrich.
6. Punch two holes above the head of your Ostrich, deep enough to hold the cloves that will serve as the bird's eye.

Insert Neck Creation

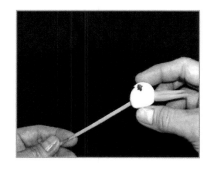

Dye bamboo skewers ahead of time before actual preparations.
You can use any type & size of skewer as desired.

1. Take the skewer you have been preparing for the neck,
2. Insert the skewer into the turnip's head to create a neck.

Carrot Web-feet

1. The easiest vegetable carving is when we talk about carrot web feet; it's been in my minds heart telling me to do my passion in carvings with fruit and vegetables like carrot and form it into some kind of bird's foot. It is found in illustrations page 16, Column A & B.
2. This time you will need more of bamboo sticks than toothpicks to secure the ostrich. It will also serve as ostrich's legs.

How to assemble the Turnip Ostrich

1. Use a bamboo skewers to emphasize the appearance of the Ostrich neck.
2. Do not use toothpick for it would not hold your turnip.
3. On your Ostrich's body, insert another two skewers on the bottom part to have it look like a real Ostrich with its thin long legs.
4. Position your Ostrich's head with its beak & neck attached, found in the photo illustration on p 48.
5. Insert the neck and the head at the body of the ostrich. Attach the cloves for the eyes, see photo picture on p. 48.
6. Proceed with putting the wings at the side of your Turnip body.
7. Follow it with the tail and secure them with toothpicks.

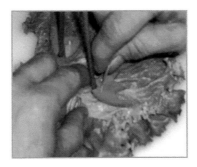

8. Your orange, potato & red beets will be cut an inch thick to serve as base; see photo illustration p. 17, Steps and procedure on how to form fruits and vegetable base for your Turnip Ostrich in the making.
9. You will need any green leafy vegetables to act as accessories to your fruits & vegetable base, to add glamour to your presentation.
10. Use paring knife, cut a small V-shape at the back of the carrot web feet, use paring knife to cut and attach a carrot web feet above the green leaves with toothpicks to hold it in place.
11. Now, it is ready to grace antipasto platters and other buffet tables.

Pineapple Bigmouth Basses

Tools

- 2 Chef Knife
- Paring Knife or
- Curved Paring Knife
- Peeler

Pineapple Bigmouth Basses
Centerpiece on cold cuts platter with garnishes

Fruits and Vegetables

- 1pc.   Fresh pineapple (any sizes)
- 1pc.   Carrots (large)
- 2pcs. Red grapes (large)
- 1pack Toothpicks (round)

Other ways to create Pineapple bigmouth basses

1. Fresh pineapple, preferably large in size and of good quality.
2. Peel off skin around the pineapple with the use of a chef's knife.
3. Create a base by cutting its bottom.
4. Use two chef's knife to cut an equal V-shape in the pineapple by making sharp edge of knife gets in contact with each other. Extract pineapple meat to form the mouth of your pineapple bass. Shown in the photo illustration.

5. Create a lip that measures an inch.
6. You have to scrape a C formation on the upper and lower insides of the fish mouth. Be extra careful with the fruit meat, you might damage the whole fish.
7. In doing so, you must use a paring knife to get good results.
8. Just like any other fish, it has to have fins and tail.

9. Carve a section on the upper back side so with at the sides of your Pineapple bigmouth bass, that section is where you situate the fins and tail. Make sure it is deep enough to accommodate them.

10. After cutting and forming the mouth after which core of the meat is removed with a V-shape formation as shown in the illustration.
11. Use paring knife to carve C-form/half moon shape below and top of the pineapple's mouth without damaging the inner meat.
12. Remove the meat by cleaning up the insides.
13. Set a side for later use.

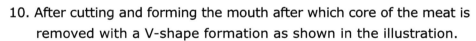

Steps to create fins and tongue

1. Select a large carrot, discard skin by using as peeler.

2. Create four slanting cuts to carrot that measures at .03–05 cm thick.

3. Just like the lemon fish fin, you can carve it like a flame shape.

   See photo illustration p. 37 (Manipulating a flame shape fins)

4. Utilize remaining carrot to produce a tongue.

5. The tongue must be smaller than the fins.

6. You will use two red grapes or maraschino cherries for the fish's eye.

7. Toothpicks will secure all body parts together, since we are not into metal bolts and screw.

How to assemble

1. The pineapple fish body first; insert carrot fins on top of the upper

   backside, again, toothpick will secure them in place.

2. You will need toothpicks to give more distinctions to the eyes,

   with red grapes or maraschino cherries on it.

3. Insert the carrot tongue inside the pineapple mouth, with

   toothpick to hold it in place. Now, it's ready to use.

4. As soon as you finish assembling all the necessary body parts,

place it on cold platters, antipasto plates and place it on center tables.

White Cabbage Lilies

Two commonly seen vegetables combined by flair to make an outward appearance of a magnificent tropical bouquet.

Red Cabbage with Turnip a Stamen

Tools

- Chef's Knife
- Paring Knife
- Peeler
- Scissors
- 2bags Bamboo Skewers
- Containers or Bowl (large)

Fruits and vegetable

- 3heads   White cabbage or red cabbage (whole)
- 2–3cups   Unflavored gelatin powder
- 1bunch   Heather leaves or any green leafy vegetables
- 1whole   Watermelon
- 1pc.   Fresh pineapple (whole)

Steps and procedure on how to make a bouquet out of cabbage lilies

1. Select a cabbage, regular in size with loose leaves. Use a chef's knife to cut off cabbages' top core by an inch to have easy access in separating leaf after leaf. As shown in the photo illustration for further guidance on how to do it the right way.

2. Place it under running water to do away with the leaves easily. As shown in the photo illustration found below, you have to cut it smaller by removing a piece of it on the top core.

3. Set aside about 40 leaves or more to create lavish cabbage bouquet.

4. It is now ready to be formed as a real looking leaf with its V-cut on the top core.

5. It is also advisable to use a scissor when forming the cabbage into a Heart shaped leaf.

6. Complete the process until you reach the desired numbers needed; to complete the bouquet.

7. Put them all in a container filled with water and let it stay in the refrigerator for a night before the actual preparation.

Stamen creation

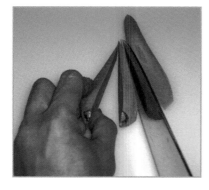

1. Use a carrot, peel and discard skin.
2. Form a "pyramid shape." from a diagonal cut using a paring knife.
3. Shave off carrots bottom to have a base, slice as plenty of stamen as required; that would match the number of heart shaped cabbage leaf you have had prepared.
4. Just like the cabbage leaf, you have to refrigerate the carrot stamen and put it in a bowl of water.

5. On page seven you can find how it is to dye bamboo skewers, just follow the steps.
6. Presuming you had the bamboo skewers in handy, insert it on the Cabbage's hard-core to form a stem. Let the skewer pass through a bit longer, enough to hold the carrot stamen just above it.
7. It is shown below, the cabbage leaf should face skyward to make it looks more real than reel.

Steps to follow on how to assemble

1. How to dye bamboo skewers with green colors, see instruction on page 7
2. Unflavored gelatin preparation, see instruction on page 8.
3. How to prepare the flower vase is on page 7.
4. Add heather leaves to the flower vase to add up glamour.

5. Dip each leaf into the gelatin solution until leaf is fully covered. Let it drip for a second, them arrange it straight to your flower vase.
6. When doing a floral arrangement, be confident that the finish product looks unbearably beautiful than you had imagined. That's the secret of having art as your master.

Elegant Turnip Roses

Turnip roses sitting on a center table

Tools

- Chef's Knife
- Paring Knife
- Curve Paring Knife
- Peeler
- Containers/bowl (large)

Fruits and Vegetables

- 40–50pcs. White turnips (any size)
- 1–2cups Red food coloring
- 1–2cups Yellow food coloring
- 1–2cups Purple food coloring
- 1–2cups Green food coloring
- 2-bags Green bamboo skewers 12"
- 1pc. Watermelon (seedless/regular)
- 2-3cups Unflavored gelatin powder

How to prepare Turnip Rose

1. Take a piece of white turnip, any size will do. Peel off skin and discard. This process should be done ahead of time from actual preparation.
2. Three fourth of the turnip should be shaved off by the use of a knife.

3. First row of the petal

- Start from the top, shape a line forming a C-cut in a slanting way by using a curve paring knife to maintain equal footing to your first row of the petal form, without damaging the entire fruit meat.
- Repeat the process to the other side to complete the petal form.
- Always remove excess meat so you will have a visual picture of your progress, in creating a rose petal out of your turnip fruit.

4. Second row of the petals

- To reach an authentic floral effect, you must start carving from the top at an alternate position.

5. Third row of the petals

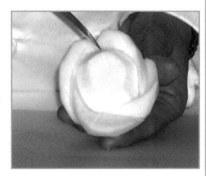

- Follow the same procedure as above, until you reach the end part of the turnip.
6. The last row will determine the exact profile of your rose turnip, and from there you can see if you had proportioned it to look like a real rose.
7. Once done carving, set them aside and divide it all into as many colors you have in mind, rose's colors are optional.

- Soak white turnip roses into colors of your choice and leave it refrigerated overnight. Make sure they are kept in separate containers with their respective color preference.
- 3 liters of water
- 1 cup food coloring about any color

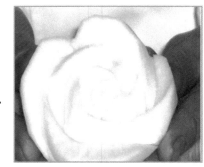

Note:

1. How to dye bamboo skewers with green colors, see instruction on p. 7.
2. Preparation of unflavored gelatin, see instruction on p. 8.
3. Flower vase preparation, see instruction on p. 7.
4. Add heather leaves around the flower vase.

Simple steps to assemble elegant Rose display

1. Put colored turnip roses on trays separately. Wash it with water for a few seconds and let dry. Use clean cloth or strainers to let colors drip.
2. Attach turnip rose on green bamboo skewers one at a time. Be reminded toothpicks would not hold a turnip rose that is why we need a skewer on heavier fruits. You can double up the skewers if Turnip is much too heavy.
3. Dip turnip rose into the gelatin solution and make sure it is fully covered. Let gelatin drip before you put it into final arrangement.
4. You can now take pride in your creation and display it on buffet tables as centerpiece.

Cucumber Star Flowers

Tools

- Chef's Knife
- Paring Knife
- Curve Paring Knife
- Containers/bowls (large)

Necessary fruit and Vegetable needed

- At least 25pcs.   Cucumber (medium)
- 50pcs.   Bamboo skewers (green) 12" or
- 2bags   Bamboo skewers 12" (100pcs. in a bag)
- 3 to 4 bunches   Fresh parsley leaf or any leaf
- 1pc.   Fresh pineapple
- 1pc.   Watermelon (regular/seedless)
- 3cups   Unflavored gelatin powder

Procedure and Preparation

Prepare a large container with cold water. Make sure there will be enough space for the starflowers to spread out their leaves.

1. Select a cucumber to create a starflower of any size.
2. Use a chef knife to cut the cucumber in halves.

3. After cutting the cucumber into two, use a paring knife to manipulate a sleek V-cut around the cucumber in about five to six equal proportion. That cut would enhance a petal formation on your cucumber.

4. Along the sides of the cut cucumber, try removing the skin without puncturing the inner connection between its meat.
5. Continue carvings the rest of the cucumber until you reach 50 or more Cucumber starflowers
6. After creating a cucumber starflower, place it inside the water filled container. Refrigerate for at least two consecutive nights. It would make the skin separate from the cucumber without cutting away the connections between the meat and skin.

Steps on how to assemble

1. How to dye bamboo skewers is found on page 7.

2. Preparation of unflavored gelatin on page 8.

3. Watermelon vase is on page 7.

4. As you gather all necessary materials found on the list above, you can now add the heather leaves or any leaf around the watermelon vase.

5. Bring about the cucumber starflowers, dry them off in a tray without damaging every petal form.

6. Attach green bamboo skewers at the bottom of starflowers one by one.
   If cucumber starflower is heavy, add more green skewers enough to hold it.

7. Dip in gelatin solution; make sure the whole flower is fully covered. Let it drip for a few second and arrange them directly to your watermelon vase.

8. Once you have completed the actual formation and established all fifty pieces of cucumber Starflowers; then bring it in the open for final scrutiny.

9. Buffet tables are dying to have your unique cucumber starflowers.

Zucchin Tulip Flowers

Tools

- Chef's Knife
- Paring Knife
- Curve Paring Knife
- Peeler
- Containers/bowl (large)

Fruits and Vegetables needed

- 20pcs.   Zucchini flower
- 3–4pcs.   Carrot (regular)
- 2-bags   Bamboo skewers 12" (100pcs. in a bag)
- 1pc.   Fresh pineapple
- 1pc.   Watermelon (seedless/regular)
- 3cups   Unflavored gelatin powder
- 1pack   Toothpicks (round)
- Any green leafy vegetables

Steps and procedure of preparation

Prepare 20 pieces of zucchini vegetable to form 40 pieces of zucchini tulip flowers, a large sized container of which is water filled with enough space for the tulip flowers.

1. Use a piece of zucchini in good quality, without skin bruises.

2. With a knife, cut the stem of the zucchini.

3. Use the top and bottom parts of the zucchini, to make two individual Tulips flower. Carve the skin of the zucchini to form petals.

4. Use a curve paring knife to slice the skin in a downward manner making sure intervals are even and not overlapping with each other, to avoid damaging final form.

5. Give your zucchini a little twist to disintegrate from the connection and have your tulip flower.

6. Set it aside in water filled container.

7. You will be able to make 40 pieces of tulip flowers out of the twenty pieces of zucchini. So it is wise to use a much bigger container.

8. Soak your zucchini tulip flowers

9. Soak the zucchini tulip flower and let it stay for a night in the refrigerator.

10. It would be ready for the next day.

11. Prepare the carrot stamen on the same day, see instruction on page 55.

Steps on how to assemble

1. Since instruction on how to dye bamboo skewers is found on page seven; we will then skip this topic so with the preparation of the gelatin solution and proceed with the next step.
2. Instruction on how to assemble a watermelon flower vase is also on page eight. All you have to do is arrange the heather leaves along the sides of your watermelon flower vase.
3. Soaking your zucchini is necessary to have it form into a blooming flower like the one on the picture below.
4. Remove your zucchini flowers from the water without breaking their respective petals, put them on trays as you dry them with a clean cloth.

5. Attach bamboo skewers on the bottom of your tulip flowers, if it's too heavy you may add skewers.
6. Let your skewers attach through the upper center of the zucchini tulip flower or you could make the tip of your skewer holds your carrot stamen to need no toothpick to hold it.
7. Carrot stamen should be positioned at the center of the zucchini tulip flowers or you can use a toothpick to hold it firmly in place.
8. Don't forget to dip the zucchini flowers into the gelatin solution making sure all parts are covered. Let it dry and arrange it the waiting watermelon vase.
9. Another attraction to buffet tables is a Zucchini Tulip Flowers.

LEEK FLOWERS

Tools

- Chef's Knife
- Peeler
- Paring Knife
- Curve Paring Knife
- Food Tray (Flat)

Fruits and Vegetable needed

- 30pcs.   Leeks (large)
- 3pcs.   Carrot (medium)
- 2bag   Green bamboo skewers 12" (100pcs. in bag)
- 1pc.   Watermelon (seedless/regular)
- 8heads   Leek leaves (top of leeks) or any leaf
- 1pc.   Pineapple

Procedure and Illustrations

1. Select a large sized leek, preferably in good quality.
2. Use knife to cut the leek's trunk and separate the top leek, the leaves.

3. Use the bottom part, the trunk to form a flower.
4. With the use of a paring knife, cut the trunk into four equal sections. Be sure to keep the trunk from breaking away, it is essential that it is intact. (See graphic illustration.)
5. You will extract small stratum from the four-sectioned part of the leek.
6. Make sure connections are integrally connected to hold it together.

7. As soon as segments are evident, you may now inset the sliced carrot.
8. Stationed the carrot on the center.
9. Use toothpicks to secure it in place.

10. As you can see the finish product as shown in the picture, set it aside for later use as you continue the same process for the other leeks.

11. With the carrot on the middle of your sectioned leek, put it upside down in trays filled with water and refrigerate for at least a night.

Procedure and Preparation

1. Dye in advance the bamboo skewers.
2. Gelatin solutions can be done while arranging your leek flowers.
3. Watermelon vase can also be done ahead of time, before actual arrangement.

How to assemble

1. If watermelon vase is ready, remove the leek flowers from the water-filled bowl.
2. Let dry the leeks and insert bamboo skewer on the base and dip in the gelatin solution.
   Make sure all parts are fully covered.
   Let it drip for a second and arrange them one by one into the watermelon vase.
3. How to dye bamboo skewers is found on page 7.
4. Preparation of unflavored gelatin on page 8.
5. Watermelon vase is on page 7.
6. As you gather all necessary materials found on the list above, you can now add the heather leaves or any leaf around the watermelon vase.
7. Bring about the cucumber starflowers, dry them off in a tray without damaging every petal form.
8. Attach green bamboo skewers at the bottom of starflowers one by one.
   If cucumber starflower is heavy, add more green skewers enough to hold it.
9. Dip in gelatin solution, make sure the whole flower is fully covered. Let it drip for a few second and arrange them directly to your watermelon vase.
10. Once you have completed the actual formation and established all fifty pieces of cucumber Starflowers; then bring it in the open for final scrutiny.
11. Buffet tables are dying to have your unique cucumber starflowers.
12. As you have organized the leek flowers into a magnificent floral arrangement, it will be more than ready to grace any buffet tables.

Onion Chrysanthemums

Jewel-toned brilliance of an elegant floral collection

Tools

- Chef's Knife
- Paring Knife or
- Curve Paring Knife
- Containers or Bowl (large)

Onions on the go

- 30pcs.   White onions (any size)
- 2bags   Bamboo skewers 12" (100 paces. in bag)
- 2cups   Red food coloring
- 2cups   Yellow food coloring
- 2cups   Purple food coloring or any food coloring
- 1pc.   Pineapple
- 1pc.   Watermelon (seedless/regular)
- 1bunch   Heather (optional)

Illustrations and Procedure

1. Use a piece of white onion, any size will do.
2. With the use of a chef's knife to cut ¼ of an inch from the top.
3. Peel off and discard onion's skin.
4. Make sure you do not puncture the white rind or inner meat.

5. After removing the upper part, sliced it into four equal sections.
6. Do not cut up to the cutthroat.

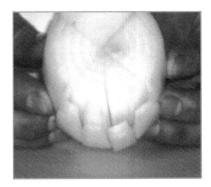

7. The four sections you have sliced, should be cut into three or for equal parts as shown in the picture.

8. Use the pointed tip of your paring knife to puncture its bottom, deep enough for your skewers.
9. Prepare deep bowl or any food containers.
10. Soak all onions in separate containers with their respective food coloring. Be sure to have it soaked for at least two consecutive nights. Change water 2x a day to remove the stinky smell and refrigerate.

- Three liters of water for every cup of food coloring.
- At least two cups of food coloring or any color of your choice.

After two days you may now form your onions into a flower

How to assemble

1. Have your skewers in handy.
2. With or without unflavored gelatin or
   The unflavored gelatin should be prepared while you arrange your onion flowers.
3. Watermelon vase can also be done in advance.
4. Arrange heather leaves or any leaf all over the bouquet until it looks more than just a bungle of leaves.
5. Take out the onion flowers from the container, wash with water to remove extra coloring. Let dry on trays
6. Insert the green skewers at the bottom of the onion.
7. And dip it in the gelatin solution until fully covered.
   Let dry for a few seconds and then arrange directly to the waiting vase.
8. Once you have completely organized at least thirty or more onion flowers, make a mental picture of how it would look as elegant as real flowers.
9. Display in buffet tables or any events that requires the beauty and expertise of fruit and vegetable carvings.

Pepper Flowers

Tools

- Chef's Knife
- Paring Knife or
- Curved Paring Knife
- Flower Cutter
- Containers/Bowl (large)

Fruits and Vegetables required

- 5pcs.   Green peppers (medium/large)
- 5pcs.   Yellow peppers (medium/large)
- 8pcs.   Red peppers (medium/large)
- 2   Bunches of green leafy vegetables
- 2bags   Green bamboo skewers
- 1pc.   Watermelon (seedless/regular)
- 2 bags   Bamboo skewer (12", 100 pcs. in a bag)
- 3cups   Unflavored gelatin powder

Procedure of preparation

1. Use eighteen or more assorted peppers in good quality.
2. Use a chef's knife to cut stem of pepper, just like the one shown in the photo illustration.

3. Position your pepper upright, cut its lobe in three equal parts without penetrating the base line so you could have it formed into a leaf.

4. After creating three equal sections, strip it into strings, make sure you do not go beyond the base and damage the peppers leafy formation.
5. Use a paring knife to establish equal strips to your pepper.

6. Fill a large container with water to soak the newly cut pepper, make sure the have enough room and space to open up.
7. You have to wait for at least 1-2 or 3three nights for your pepper to open up to perfection.

Hot to assemble your Pepper flowers

1. See instruction on p. 7, on how to dye bamboo skewers.

2. Unflavored gelatin solution on page 8.

3. Before organizing the watermelon flower vase, remember the following:

   • Use a flower cutter to mark half of the watermelon, forming it into a flower.

   • Use a washable marker to trace a flower formation on the outer skin of watermelon.

   • With a paring knife, peel off skin where you formed the flower.

   • Make three or more flower design around your watermelon vase. Floral design is optional.

   • Cut pineapple into two, also cross wise. Utilize the other half and put it in the center of your Watermelon vase. Secure it with skewer.

   • Attach more skewers at the center of the pineapple and into the watermelon.

   • Make sure you have enough skewers to hold the flower vase.

4. Arrange heather leaves or any green leaf of your choice, along the sides of flower vase until it appears like a jungle of leafy vegetables in the heart of pepper flowers.

5. Dry pepper flowers with a clean cloth and arrange them on trays.

6. Stick bamboo skewers on every pepper flower.

7. Dip it right through the gelatin solution until fully covered, let extra gelatin drip for a second before arranging them into the watermelon base.

8. Before you proceed to actual presentation, make sure your pepper flowers are virtually like a bona fide replica of real flowers, in a simple vegetable carving that enhances not only the palate but also the imagination; worthy to become centerpiece or show pieces.

Zucchini Flowers

Create a touch of spring anytime of the year, with easy to prepare zucchini vegetable flowers

Tools

- Chef Knife
- Paring Knife
- Curve Paring Knife
- Peeler
- Containers or Bowl (large)

Fruits and vegetables

- 20pcs.   Whole piece of zucchini (any size) cut in half, 40 pieces.
- 40pcs.   Green bamboo skewers or
- 2 bags   bamboo skewers 12" (100 pcs. in bag)
- 1bunch   Heather leaves or any leaves
- 1–2   Cups red food coloring
- 1–2   Cups yellow food coloring
- 1–2   Cups purple food coloring
- 1–2   Cups orange food coloring or any color of choice
- 1pc.   Pineapple (with leaves)
- 1pc.   Watermelon
- 3cups   Unflavored gelatin

Procedure of preparations

Before you prepare a zucchini flower, set aside three large bowls filled with cold colored water. A color of your choice will be of great help.

1. Select a piece of zucchini, of good quality.
2. With a chef's knife, cut zucchini into two to have two individual flowers.
3. With a paring knife, divide it into five to six equal sections forming a V-shape to create a zucchini star. Ensure an equal footing of all sides.

4. As soon as your star is visible, carefully cut away the skin without fully removing it from the meat to serve as petals.
5. Soak and dye zucchini flowers into a large container, preferably with color distinctions. Refrigerate it overnight.

Actual preparations

1. Be ready with you green skewers, dyed in advance. P 7
2. Gelatin solutions in a bowl. P 8
3. Watermelon flower vase. P 7
4. Arrange heather leaves or any leaf all over the floral vase until it looks fascinating.
   Remove zucchini flowers in the containers, wash excess colors with tap water, put them on flat trays. Be careful not to break petals.

After an overnight soaking, zucchini flowers looks amazingly real.

Petals bloom like a spring dew, and ready for attraction.

Few steps on how to assemble

1. Regard the zucchini flower and place bamboo skewer at its bottom. If the zucchini flower is too heavy add another skewer enough to hold it. Shown in the illustration.

2. Dip in gelatin solution until zucchini flower is fully covered, let extra gelatin drip for a Second; put them in the flower vase directly.

3. Once you complete the floral arrangement of zucchini flowers; you have to make sure it looks more real than interesting.

4. Display it on buffet tables or any occasions that require a centerpiece or showpieces such as fruit and vegetable carvings.

Eggplant Chihuahua

Tools

- Chef's Knife
- Paring Knife
- Curve Paring Knife
- Peeler

Fruits and Vegetables

1pc.	Eggplant (large)
2pcs.	Grapefruit
1pc.	Fresh lemon
4–5pcs.	Carrots long (Medium)
50g.	Red grapes (Small)
1pc.	Cantaloupe
1bag	Bamboo skewers (12 inch or as you desire)
1pack	Toothpick (round)

Procedure and preparation

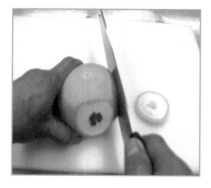

Select a grapefruit, preferably round an in good quality.

Use a chef's knife to cut two circles side by side in between the grapefruit to create eye formation.

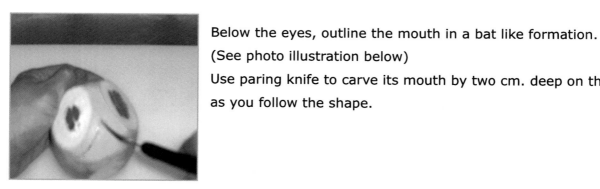

Below the eyes, outline the mouth in a bat like formation.

(See photo illustration below)

Use paring knife to carve its mouth by two cm. deep on the marked line as you follow the shape.

At the corner of the eyes, use paring knife to perform a C-cut at about four to five cm. deep; enough to insert the formed grapefruit ears.

Set aside for later use.

Use another piece of grapefruit. Eliminate an oval formation using a chef's Knife and that will serve as the ears.

Ways to form the body of a vegetable chihuahua

1. Use large eggplant of good quality.
2. Cut its stem with a chef's knife to form a stable base.
3. Cut also the bottom by an inch to form a stable base.
4. Four pieces of carrot, peeled.
5. Use carrots to have three inches long component to serve as arms and legs.
6. Make a straight cut over the tip while on the thicker part of a slant cut (see photo illustrations p24- top column) should be done to have more fitting section when connected to the eggplant.
7. Take a piece of fresh lemon, use knife cut in half, cut and slice .05 inch lemon rings to use for the creating the neck. Shown in the photo picture below column.
   While the other half use for the hat.

ASSEMBLE WHEN THROUGH WITH ARMS AND LEGS

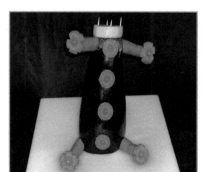

1. Attach carrot arms on top and legs on the bottom part.
2. Utilize remaining carrots to form four-rounded shape, attach it in the center.
3. Then cut other two-rounded carrots for the eyes.
4. Prepare a piece of red grapes for the nose.
5. One whole cantaloupe cut at least two cm thick. Also a lemon cut into two cross-wise for the hat.
6. To create the feet see photo illustrations p 24.

How to assemble

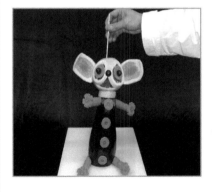

1. Use the grapefruit you prepared for the head of the Chihuahua.
2. Attach two pieces of grapefruit skin on both corners to create the ears. Use toothpicks to secure it.
3. Attach the grapefruit head on top of the eggplant. Insert skewers all the way down to the eggplant.
4. Attach the rounded carrot to the grapefruit to have a physical eye presentation. Place toothpicks on both eye to hold it in place.
   Insert two grapes, cut an inch rounded to complete the act.

5. Be sure to leave a space in between the eyes, enough for a grape to sit in as nose.
6. For final decoration, bring about the cantaloupe and the lemon on top of the grapefruit to make out the hat.
7. Display it on buffet tables, cheese and wine bars or any occasions that needs and artful carving of fruits and vegetables.
8. Display in buffet, cheese and wine display, or any events.

Pango's Giant Mouse

Centerpiece, sitting around an elegant fruit display saying.
"Hello to all, have a good party."

Pango's Giant Mouse in a
well-dressed mood.

Tools

- Chef's Knife
- Paring Knife
- V Shape Carving tool 3/8 inch
- Peeler

Fruits and Vegetable

- 1 pc.   Honeydew melon round (medium)
- 1 pc.   Honeydew melon oval (large)
- 1 pc.   Cantaloupe melon (large)
- 4 pcs.   Yellow squash regular size
- 1 pc.   Carrots (large)
- 2 pcs.   Red or Black grapes (large)
- 2 pcs.   Maraschino cherries
- 1 pc.   Lemon or Fresh orange
- 1 pc.   Eggplant (large)
- 1 pc.   Skin of watermelon or any fruit (for hat)
- 1 bag   Bamboo skewers 12" (100 pcs. in a bag)
- 1 pack Toothpicks, round shape

Steps and Procedure on how to create a Melon Ears

1. Choose cantaloupes melon; use a chef's knife to slice the skin off at about .05 inch thick to serve as the ears.
2. Use a washable marker or a sketch carving tool, draw a pointed oval shape at the back of the melon's skin.

3. Flip it over sideways creating a V-shape to have easy access to the lines.
4. Use a curve paring knife to cut away the V-form along the sides. Shown in the illustration.

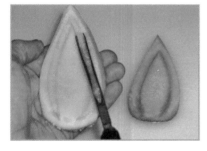

5. Flip it over to show the touch of its meat.
6. Then, use V Shape Carving tool 3/8 inch, to carve the meat at the edge of the melon skin to create a pointed oval shape to form ears.

Head Preparation
Steps on how to create the head

1. Use a large carrot, skinned clean.
2. Cut two-rounded slice, at least .04 cm thick, insert the carrot in between the melon to form the eyes, toothpicks to hold
3. Insert the melon ears at the corner side of the melon head, toothpicks to hold.
4. Prepare three pieces of red or black grapes use a knife to cut an inch; attach it at the top of the round carrots to form pupils to create the eyes. Toothpicks to hold.
5. The other piece of red grapes, use toothpick to hold and insert at the center of the eyes, do not go through, then attach the grapes in the middle to form the nose.
6. Take a piece of lemon, cut into two cross wise, attach at the top of the watermelons skin using a skewer to hold, if long break it.

7. The remaining carrots will be cut & sliced oval shape at .04 thick for the tongue, use toothpick to hold.

8. Two maraschino cherries shall be cut into two, also cross wise for the buttons.

Preparation on how to assemble the body

1. Choose an oblong sized melon for the body (large).
2. Cut at .05 inch thick for the base.
3. Attach yellow squash to form the arms and legs. Use toothpicks to hold.
4. Attach carrot hands and feet at the tip of each squash.
5. Use an eggplant, a knife to it by an inch thick to create the neck.
6. Insert the rounded eggplant at the top of the melon's body.
7. Take two whole maraschino cherries, use paring knife and cut it in halves.
   Attach maraschino cherries at the center of the melon to create buttons.
   Use toothpicks to hold it in place, as shown in the photo illustrations.

How to assemble

1. Take the melon's head attach it at the top of the melon's body, insert bamboo skewers on top of the Lemon/Orange fruit to create the hat.
2. To complete the mouse, do not forget to attach the carrot tongue
3. Display Pango's Giant Mouse in any special events or occasions that requires showpiece or centerpiece of that sort.

Tomato Rose

Tomato rose decoration atop grilled zucchini
with it's delicious garnishing.

Tools

- Curve Paring Knife
- Paring Knife

Ingredient

1pc.   Tomato Large size or any colors

How to make a tomato rose

1. Ripe tomato but not tender.
2. Cut the bottom part to create a base by cm. cut..
3. Use a paring knife to cut skin sideways.

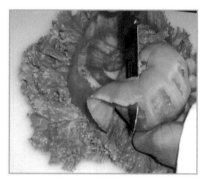

4. Continue the process until your knife will reach the bottom part.

5. Use the tomato skin and roll it together until it will form into a rose.
6. It would be easy to make a rose out of tomato skin than do a rose by carving.

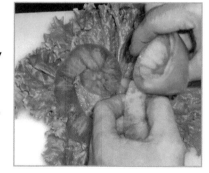

7. It is by rolling it together and using the imaginative side of your mind to produce that elegant looking rose from a tomato skin.
8. This type of design can be put together with any type of salad garnishing in dinner plates, platters, or salad bowl.

Tomato Star Flower

Tomato starflower sitting at the center of a marinated mushroom with garnishing on an antipasto oval platter with decorations

Tools

- Chef Knife
- Curve Paring Knife
- Paring Knife

Ingredient

1pc. Tomato Large size or any colors

Procedure and preparation

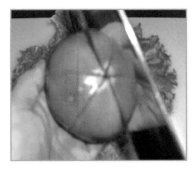

1. Ripe tomato but not tender and of good quality.
2. With a chef knife, start slicing at the center of the tomato.
   Hit the skin at least .03–.04 cm deep.
   Careful not to slice all through its bottom as you section it into six equal parts.

3. By using a curve paring knife, carve the center of each equal portion.
   An elongated triangle, a semi-pyramid to form the petals of the tomato star flower, be careful do not go through.

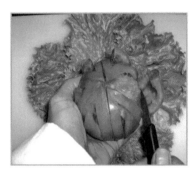

4. Use a paring knife to deepen the cut, deep enough for the skin to open up away from the meat without breaking.

5. Spread the equally lacerated tomato skin without damaging the tender fruit to always have a distinct floral formation.

6. Have it look like a star, push with a little pressure using your finger to move the pyramid shaped skin forward, and in that manner you will have a petal form from tomato skin alone.
7. You can use this type of floral tomato magic to grace antipasto platters and other salad bowls. See picture illustration on page 85.

Edited by: Rosalie Rosaliah Tambis

A.K.A Touch

A Filipino Artist – Alfredo Tambis Pango

Pango is a Chef Garde Manger and a creative artist. With him is his favorite fruit and vegetable carving to be displayed at any occasions or events, that is the Pango's Giant Mouse. Buffet tables, Antipasto Bars, Cheese and Wine Display corner, Exotic Caribbean fruit buffet, Bars/bat Mitzvahs, Baptismal events, Weddings and many other occasions that need the masterpiece of an artful design using simple fruits and vegetables found in your kitchen will appear as magic in Pango's hands. That is one gargantuan reason why Pango has created a masterpiece to entice not just the palate but the visual apparatus, as well; it is also a way of saying thank you to all who have had given him the support and the encouragement . . .

Thank you,